DIGITAL MARKETING FOR DOCTORS

28 PROVEN STRATEGIES FOR BUSY DOCTORS

DIBAKAR BALA

Copyright © Dibakar Bala
All Rights Reserved.

ISBN 978-1-63781-948-7

This book has been published with all efforts taken to make the material error-free after the consent of the author. However, the author and the publisher do not assume and hereby disclaim any liability to any party for any loss, damage, or disruption caused by errors or omissions, whether such errors or omissions result from negligence, accident, or any other cause.

While every effort has been made to avoid any mistake or omission, this publication is being sold on the condition and understanding that neither the author nor the publishers or printers would be liable in any manner to any person by reason of any mistake or omission in this publication or for any action taken or omitted to be taken or advice rendered or accepted on the basis of this work. For any defect in printing or binding the publishers will be liable only to replace the defective copy by another copy of this work then available.

Dedicated to my Mother (Sabita Bala) who have always been supportive about my choices in life.

Contents

Preface   *vii*

1. Digital Marketing For A Doctor Is More Like Personal Branding   1
2. Ideal Patient Persona Would Replace Ideal Buyer Persona   2
3. 21st Century & Personal Branding Has Something In Common : Videos   4
4. Start With What's Comfortable For You : Video, Audio, Text   5
5. Go Omni-channel With Your Healthcare Content Distribution   6
6. People Will Judge Your Online Presence   7
7. Integrate Online Appointment Scheduling With Your Website   8
8. Conversion Rate Optimization Is A Real Thing   9
9. Transformational Case Study Works Best In Healthcare Digital Marketing   10
10. Attach Google Map Pin Of Your Clinic Everywhere   11
11. Dedicated Phone Number For Appointment Booking   12
12. Local Seo & Google My Business   13
13. Messenger Bot, Whatsapp Bot, Alexa Skills, Etc.   15
14. Online Reputation Management   16

Contents

15. Traditional Seo	17
16. Directory Listing	18
17. Stop Relying On Third Party Platforms For Patients	19
18. Capture Inbound Leads Using Lead Magnets	20
19. Create Micro Video Content	21
20. Promote Your Short Videos	22
21. Retargeting & Remarketing	23
22. Email Funnels	24
23. Google Phone Call Ads	25
24. Leverage Opn	26
25. Be Active On Forums Like Quora	27
26. Network On Linkedin To Get Speaking Gigs	28
27. Recommended Tools For Doctors	29
28. Consistency Is The Key	30
Conclusion	31

Preface

Digital Marketing for Doctors is more crucial than ever. Did you know that 92% of patients living in Urban locations always search for the Doctor's Name on Google before scheduling an Appointment?

In this Book, I am going to share with you my Complete Roadmap of strategizing a Digital Marketing Campaign for a Busy Professional Doctor just like you.

CHAPTER ONE

Digital Marketing for a Doctor is more like Personal Branding

Although, we can borrow a lot of ideas from Healthcare Digital Marketing Campaigns. Yet, Healthcare Organizations like Hospitals are not the same as doctors or physicians.

While Hospitals & Nursing Homes are Businesses, Doctors are individuals. Thereby, making the whole campaign design a lot more dependent on the doctor himself/herself.

CHAPTER TWO

Ideal Patient Persona would replace ideal buyer persona

In general, when we start to think about designing any Online Marketing Campaign, we look at our Target Audience and create an Ideal Buyer Persona out of it.

These personas are quite hypothetical and based on market research and/or competitor analysis.

For Doctors, this process gets a lot easier as we most probably know a lot about our ideal patient based on our history of patient data.

But while creating the ideal patient persona, make sure not to use assumptions just because you specialize in certain disease.

For example, if you are a Nutritionist, do not simply say that 'everyone' is your potential client. Look at your last 12 months patient list and try to find a pattern in it.

Are you getting approached mostly by men, or are they women? What is the median age for all such cases? What income bracket do they belong? Do they live near your clinic? How many were international clients?

List out all these findings and you now have a hypothetical ideal patient profile who might be a pregnant women aged 30 and is suffering from obesity.

CHAPTER THREE

21st Century & Personal Branding has something in Common : Videos

21st Century is the Century of Videos. You just can't deny the amount of content being uploaded and consumed on the internet in the form of videos.

Add the additional factor of Personal Branding and you just cannot ignore Videos whatsoever.

I am an extremely introverted person myself and I completely go off the script every time I start the camera.

Still out of necessity I started making Videos and now my 3 YouTube Channels collectively has got something close to a thousand subscribers.

CHAPTER FOUR

Start with what's comfortable for you : Video, Audio, Text

Blogging has always been a successful method of sharing information.

Videos are clearly trending in 2021. But not everyone is comfortable in front of the Camera.

Podcasting is another great platform for anybody who wants to share their knowledge and don't have the time or patience to write a long form article.

Bottom of the line, you need to find a way of sharing your knowledge that is most comfortable to you.

CHAPTER FIVE

Go Omni-Channel with your Healthcare Content Distribution

Just because you wrote a 1000 word article about 'how to avoid male pattern baldness?" doesn't mean you should stop there.

Create a Graphic Slide out of your post and share it on Instagram. Convert the Graphics into a PDF and upload it as a Document on Linkedin.

Make a Twitter Thread out of the whole article. Record a Podcast episode reading out the whole article.

Lastly, if you can and you definitely should create a Video on YouTube summarizing the whole Article.

That's how you can repurpose your single content and generate a lot of eyeballs for it across multiple platforms.

CHAPTER SIX

People will judge your Online Presence

We live in a world were people judge you by your looks. Same happens with your social media and website.

If you have a Website, make sure it looks minimal & professional in design.

Don't overdo elements unnecessarily just to make it look better than your competitors.

CHAPTER SEVEN

Integrate Online Appointment Scheduling with your Website

Appointment Scheduling is the equivalent of Lead Generation when it comes to Doctors.

Use Free Appointment Scheduling Software like Calendly and integrate it cleverly into your website.

Make sure it is easily accessible for every website visitor. Ideally, make it a sticky button or a floating bar on every web page of your site.

CHAPTER EIGHT

Conversion Rate Optimization is a Real Thing

CRO or Conversion Rate Optimization is the art of getting more conversions out of your existing website traffic.

Free Tools like Google Optimize are the industry standard for conducting any CRO campaign.

If you cannot hire a CRO Expert, follow some best practices like :- improving the landing page copy, integrate live chat feature, testimonials, etc.

CHAPTER NINE

Transformational Case Study works best in Healthcare Digital Marketing

If there is one best strategy we can borrow from healthcare marketing, it would be 'Case Studies' of patient transformation.

Medical Businesses are using this strategy ever since Print Advertisements came into picture.

Basically you need to keep pictures & videos of your patients before & after their treatment and present them as case studies to your future prospects.

IMPORTANT :- Make sure to respect your patient's privacy as well. Things can go really bad if you do not take proper permissions before publishing any such photos & videos.

CHAPTER TEN

Attach Google Map Pin of your Clinic everywhere

People today prefer to use GPS while locating anything on the road. Gone are the days when we used to ask local shopkeepers for the best route to reach a location.

What is even more interesting is that people now check the navigation route from their own place to the doctor's clinic even before they decide to book an appointment.

Thus, you must export your Google Map Location Pin for your Clinic and embed it everywhere possible including your website & facebook page.

CHAPTER ELEVEN

Dedicated Phone Number for Appointment Booking

Even though you have got an Appointment Scheduling software working for you 24 hours X 365 Days. Some people would just like to get on a Phone Call directly.

Make sure you get a phone number dedicated just for patient calls. Also, I would encourage you to promote it on every Social Media Platform and through Online Advertisements (more details about this in next few points).

CHAPTER TWELVE

Local SEO & Google My Business

By now you might already know about Google My Business. You might even have a verified Business Profile on GMB.

But, do you rank #1 for local search queries like "best psychiatrist in New York" or "Best Denstist in Los Angeles".

Enter 'Local SEO'.

Local SEO is a completely different thing when compared with Traditional SEO.

I made a Complete Guide about Local SEO. You might want to read it if you want an in-depth knowledge about optimizing your Google My Business.

To put it simply, three major factors that has an effect on Local SEO rankings are :- proximity, popularity & relevance.

Proximity is how far is your clinic from the patient's location who is performing the search.

Popularity is measured based on the number of positive reviews you have got on your GMB profile.

Relevance is nothing but NAP citations. NAP stands for Name Address Phone Number and citations are nothing but local listing of your business on other directories apart from Google My Business.

As SEO, we cannot influence the Proximity factor of Google My Business listing a lot. But, we can definitely influence the number of reviews by requesting our existing and future patients to leave an honest review on GMB about their experience.

NAP citation is another extremely crucial factor that we can influence by listing our clinic on multiple online local business listing directories.

CHAPTER THIRTEEN

Messenger Bot, WhatsApp Bot, Alexa Skills, etc.

Bots are the future of AI based Digital Marketing. It sure requires a lot of skill to build a Chatbot or Voice App.

Yet, it is better to invest in something like a Chatbot which will only become more prevalent in the coming future.

There are many online platforms like mobilemonkey, dialogflow, etc that can help you build your bots.

You can integrate your bot on multiple platforms including Facebook Messenger, WhatsApp Business, Website, Google Actions & Amazon Alexa.

In 2019, I won a National Tech innovation competition just by making a Voice App Bot.

CHAPTER FOURTEEN

Online Reputation Management

Online Reputation Management or ORM as we call it in Digital Marketing is quintessential for Doctors & Physicians.

People will either choose you or someone else based on how many negative reviews they have got over you.

ORM is the art of controlling these negative reviews by influencing or negotiating with the reviewer across the table.

Even if we can convert or get rid of 50% of all the negative reviews we get, it will bring in a lot more patients on our way! Ultimately effecting our Annual Revenue & Profit Margins.

CHAPTER FIFTEEN

Traditional SEO

Fake Digital Marketing Agencies have ruined the reputation for Traditional SEO.

Reality is that it still works extremely well if done correctly.

Infact, I wouldn't be publishing this piece of content if SEO was not effective.

Traditional SEO was effective and will always remain effective as long as People have questions they cannot answer themselves.

CHAPTER SIXTEEN

Directory Listing

Directory Listing is actually treated by many SEO experts as a Link Building technique.

But, Doctors can use it as a tool for improving their Personal Brand as well.

Most Directory Listings are heavily funded companies who have teams dedicated for improving their Search Engine Rankings.

Needless to say, patients often end up looking for doctors on these platforms after going through a regular Google Search.

You should definitely try to outrank these directory pages with your own website. But, unless you outrank them, it is always advisable to leverage them.

Join as many business listing websites as possible and add your correct clinic details with phone number in all of them.

This will benefit in three ways :- improve online visibility, pass ranking signal to Google My Business Listing (NAP Citation) and might get you a backlink if the listing site allows a link addition.

CHAPTER SEVENTEEN

Stop Relying on third party platforms for patients

If you are a Doctor in India, most of your patients might be coming from platforms like Practo.

Same can be said about similar international third party platforms as well.

But, relying on these platforms forever is a recipe for disaster. If they go out of business or if they delete your profile for any reason, you could be back to zero in a single moment.

Although it is definitely advisable to improve your profile on such third party online doctor consultancy sites. But, do on ignore your personal website and Social Media just because these are giving you better performance today.

CHAPTER EIGHTEEN

Capture inbound leads using Lead Magnets

Lead Magnets are valuable pieces of Content that you would be willing to give away for free in return of someone's name email and phone number.

You might have come across many such lead magnets on the internet where you submitted your name and email in a web-based form to access ebook or training.

You could do the same and use them intelligently on your website pages that gets traffic from Google or Social Media.

You may even use Content Upgrades like 'PDF checklist' at the end of your Blog Articles to capture email ids of your website visitors.

CHAPTER NINETEEN

Create Micro Video Content

Contrary to popular belief, people do like in-depth content. Be it Blog Articles or Videos, your audience will love it when they get all the required information from start to finish in a single place.

Now you might be wondering, if that's true why do people think that long videos aren't effective.

Because the real reason is not the length of the video clip. Nobody likes a Boring Video. And, to keep a lengthy video engaging throughout is a skill in itself.

Thus, learn to create shorter a.k.a. Micro Videos as well.

Due to being short in length, these videos are easier to watch even if they are boring.

Consider this :- What would you like to choose? What a Boring Movie of 3 Hours? Or, a Boring Commercial of 30 Seconds?

CHAPTER TWENTY

Promote your Short Videos

Ever heard of Hope Marketing?

It is a way of Marketing where you Create Killer Quality Content and wait with patience for the Audience to find it.

It might work for you once you have built an audience who would share your content with their friends & followers.

But, ideally, it is not going to happen unless you strategically promote across multiple platforms.

So, if you have created shorter videos which are quick and easy to watch, promote them to your target audience with video view ads (facebook).

These ads are really cheap and can help in building trust about you among your audience.

CHAPTER TWENTY-ONE

Retargeting & Remarketing

Let's assume, you have been creating short videos and promoting them to your target audience.

People have watched your videos. But, now you don't know how to leverage the trust you've built in them.

Introducing "Remarketing"

Remarketing is a technique where you can marketing your products again to the same audience again.

But, to do this, you need to track who saw your earlier content first.

Well, let's just say, it is easier than ever to run remarketing campaigns thanks to various tracking codes used by Online Advertising Platforms.

You have Facebook Pixel, Google Tracking Code, etc. through which you can track website visits (blog article included).

You can even target your existing Instagram & Facebook Page Followers & target those who have watched your earlier videos.

CHAPTER TWENTY-TWO

Email Funnels

Funnels are another way of building trust and credibility by drip feeding your content to your audience.

Email Funnels are a series of Emails which are designed with a clear objective & end goal in vision.

If you are planning to pitch a regular check-up, you first need to establish yourself as an authority.

You may begin with a Free Ebook, followed by an Email about your Personal Life & how you ended up being a Doctor, then share some case studies of your past client and finally pitch your service in a sequence of emails.

Email Funnel is a complete independent field of digital marketing just like seo, facebook ads, google ads, etc.

CHAPTER TWENTY-THREE

Google Phone Call Ads

You must have come across Google Search Ads while using Google.

Some of these ads won't open up a website upon clicking.

They'll instead open up your dialer with a phone number pre-filled in it for you to give a call.

These are known as Google Call Ads and are highly effective for Doctors.

If you learn the art of extensive keyword research, you can start getting Appointment Scheduling Calls from Day 1.

The only problem with Google Ad is 'Money'. Search Ads on Google are quite expensive.

But, as we all know, fortune favors the brave.

If you are okay with spending initially, once optimized from the conversion data, nothing worse as good as Google Search Ads.

CHAPTER TWENTY-FOUR

Leverage OPN

OPN or Other People's Network is a great asset when you are low on marketing budget.

As a Doctor, you definitely have friends who would be happy to refer you to their patients.

You may even pitch them for a shared instagram live where you can share your advice with their audience.

Leveraging other people's network is a skill and takes a lot of time to learn.

CHAPTER TWENTY-FIVE

Be Active on Forums like Quora

Doctors are helpful by nature. And, Quora is the best place for Doctors who are both helpful & knowledgeable.

Find questions and topics which you can answer and simply share your opinion about them.

Do not just try to promote your website or products without providing any value.

Quora moderators frown upon such acts of spamming and will eventually delete your answers once they catch a trail.

CHAPTER TWENTY-SIX

Network on Linkedin to get Speaking Gigs

Linkedin is the holy grail of B2B networking.

Can definitely work for Doctors as well if you know how to use the Search Functionality.

Linkedin probably has one of the best Search Function across all other social media.

Linkedin gets you a ton of filtering options where you can choose industry, place of work, location and everything in between.

Once you Connect with these industry experts, make sure to provide value first before asking for something in return.

Eventually, you get to leverage their Network (OPN) by landing speaking opportunity & guest posts.

CHAPTER TWENTY-SEVEN

Recommended Tools for Doctors

Assuming that you as a Doctor aren't much into tech & Creativity, following are the tools I recommend every doctor :-

Canva is hands down the best place to design Posters & Images for Social Media

Inshot is a great Mobile Friendly Video Editing Tool where you can export your content without any watermark. (Although, Inshot hides this option in settings)

Use Facebook Ads Library to spy on your competitor's Ads. Do not copy the Ad Creative from the Library.

Rather, get inspired from their work and try to replicate the idea behind it.

If you want to get serious about SEO, definitely invest in AHREF. It is my favourite tool for Off Page SEO.

Although, since I am a full time digital marketer, I use more than 20 such paid Tools regularly.

StatusBrew is a Social Media Scheduler. Doctors are busy in general. And posting content on a regular basis is tough for almost anybody.

These schedulers can help you schedule content for the entire week/month on a single weekend.

CHAPTER TWENTY-EIGHT

Consistency is the Key

Last and Definitely not the least, Be Consistent.

No matter how hard you try, things will not work out in your favour in the first go.

It takes years for a Digital Marketer to become good at his craft.

It would definitely take you some time to gain traction for your efforts.

What generally happens is doctors would start putting out content and then eventually after 1-2 weeks they give up.

If there's anything I have learnt over the years is the fact that you cannot base your actions on your outcomes..

Just ignore the number of likes/comments/followers/subscribers and put out content because you Care.

Care is the Biggest element Online. Not everyone care about their audience.

And if you Care about them, even 1 single view will convert into your customer once they find your content :)

Conclusion

In this Book I have tried introducing you to various digital marketing strategies which you can use as a Doctor. Each of these 28 Strategies are so Deep that they could have their own Book.

If you need help with your Marketing, reach out to me at **hello@dibakarbala.com**

www.ingramcontent.com/pod-product-compliance
Lightning Source LLC
Chambersburg PA
CBHW021548200526
45163CB00016B/3079